Fine Art Studio
Watercolor

By Mary Iverson

Silver Dolphin

Silver Dolphin Books
An imprint of the Advantage Publishers Group
5880 Oberlin Drive, San Diego, CA 92121-4794
www.silverdolphinbooks.com

Text copyright © 2006 by becker&mayer!

Fine Art Studio: Watercolor is produced by becker&mayer!,
Bellevue, Washington
www.beckermayer.com

If you have questions or comments about this product, send e-mail to
infobm@beckermayer.com

ISBN-13: 978-1-59223-650-3
ISBN-10: 1-59223-650-2

Produced, manufactured, and assembled in China.

3 4 5 11 10 09 08 07

06392

Edited by Nancy Waddell
Written and illustrated by Mary Iverson
Art direction by Eddee Helms
Designed by Eddee Helms
Packaging design by Scott Westgard and Eddee Helms
Product development by Lillis Taylor and Lauren Saint
Production management by Katie Stephens

Image Credits

Every effort has been made to correctly attribute all the material reproduced
in this book. We will be happy to correct any errors in future editions.

Page 3: Cave painting of lions, *Panneau des Lions,* courtesy of and
document elaborated with the support of the French Ministry of Culture and
Communication, Regional Direction for Cultural Affairs-Rhône-Alpes, Regional
Department of Archaeology.

Page 4: Cave painting of bear, *Les Ours Rouges,* courtesy of and document
elaborated with the support of the French Ministry of Culture and
Communication, Regional Direction for Cultural Affairs-Rhône-Alpes, Regional
Department of Archaeology. Papyrus painting, detail from the Book of the
Dead depicting the deceased and his wife with garlands of flowers, Egyptian,
19th Dynasty, image from the Bridgeman Art Library. Japanese landscape
painting from istockphoto.com.

Page 5: Illuminated manuscript from clipart.com. Joseph Mallord William
Turner, *The Burning of the Houses of Parliament,* 1834, photo credit: Tate
Gallery, London / Art Resource, New York. Used with permission.

Page 14: Carol Mansfield, *Sunflower.* Paul Klee, *Versunkene Landschaft,*
Zentrum Paul Klee / Artists Rights Society (ARS), New York, photo credit:
Museum Folkwang Essen, Germany. Used with permission.

Page 20: Georgia O'Keeffe, *Evening Star No. VI,* Georgia O'Keeffe
Foundation / Artists Rights Society (ARS), New York, photo credit: Georgia
O'Keeffe Museum, Santa Fe, New Mexico / Art Resource, New York. Used
with permission.

Page 24: Painting by Beatrix Potter © Frederick Warne & Co. Ltd., 2005.
Cover from *The Tale of Peter Rabbit* by Beatrix Potter © Frederick Warne & Co.
Ltd., 1902, 2002. Reproduced with permission by Frederick Warne & Co., Ltd.

Page 28: John Singer Sargent, *The Grand Canal, Venice* © 1902, Courtesy of
the Fogg Art Museum, Harvard University Art Museums, Bequest of Grenville
L. Winthrop, 1943.313. Photo by Allan Macintyre. Used with permission.

Page 34: Mary Cassatt, *Self-portrait,* photo credit: National Portrait Gallery,
Smithsonian Institution / Art Resource, New York. Used with permission;
Photo of Mary Cassatt, Courtesy of the Pennsylvania Academy of the Fine
Arts, Philadelphia, Archives. Baroni and Gardelli, photographers. Mary Cassatt.
Carte de visite, albumen print, ca. 1872.

What Is Watercolor?

Since the beginning of recorded history, artists have used painting to express thoughts, tell stories, and beautify the world. Paintings have been made on all sorts of surfaces, from cave walls to the finest papers.

Watercolor painting is a technique that uses water-soluble paint, usually on paper. It can also be applied to other surfaces, such as plaster, stone, cardboard, and fabric. It is unique because it is simple to use, requires few supplies, and is portable. To make a watercolor painting, you don't need a big, fancy studio with large easels, canvases, oils, and solvents. The only materials you need are paints, brushes, water, and a piece of paper. This makes watercolor the perfect medium to carry into the world to create landscape paintings, record adventures in a travel diary, make close-up studies of the natural world, or experiment with colors and textures. Many famous artists have used watercolors for just these reasons.

Georgia O'Keeffe, who is well known for her large, detailed oil paintings of flowers, used watercolors to record bold, colorful impressions of natural events such as a sunset or a star shining in the sky. John Singer Sargent is famous for his portrait paintings in oil, but his secret passion was watercolor. He made watercolor sketches of cities he visited on his travels. Beatrix Potter, author of the children's book *The Tale of Peter Rabbit*, began making watercolor studies in nature as a young girl. Many of the characters in her books were based on her detailed watercolors.

Table of Contents

The Development of Watercolor Painting

Cave Painters

Prehistoric artists discovered that pigments made from ground-up rocks and burned sticks were lightfast, which means that they keep their color over time. Because they mixed these colored pigments in water, their paintings can be considered watercolors.

There are four basic colors in all prehistoric cave paintings: black, yellow, red, and brown. Black was made from carbon, which was obtained from burned wood. Yellow and red came from special rock deposits. Mixing black, yellow, and red pigments together made brown. By some accounts, cave artists traveled up to 25 miles to obtain the red rocks (what we now call iron oxide) for their dark red pigments.

STICKY SITUATIONS
Cave painters used saliva to make the paint stick to the wall.

Egypt

Long after the time of the prehistoric cave painters, watercolor came back on the scene when paper was invented in Egypt, around 3000 BC.

Paper allowed the Egyptians to write messages on something lightweight, so they didn't have to lug around heavy stone tablets anymore. The Egyptians wrote and illustrated stories on scrolls of papyrus—a type of textured paper made out of the stalks of the papyrus plant. They used watercolors to paint the pictures.

Like the cave painters, ancient Egyptians made their paints out of natural materials like rocks and burned wood. However, the Egyptians had more exotic materials available to them through trade with other countries around the Mediterranean and along the Nile River. They made bright colors out of minerals and gemstones—blue came from azurite, red from cinnabar, and green from malachite.

China and Japan

The next place where watercolor painting flourished was in the Far East, in China and Japan. In the second century BC, papermaking became an art form. Chinese artisans created paper out of silk and other soft fibers. Because of the smooth quality of this new paper, watercolor could be used in a more flowing style. The watercolor paintings from China and Japan depicted soft, misty landscapes. This type of painting would have been impossible to do on rough papyrus paper.

J. M. W. Turner, *The Burning of the Houses of Parliament*, 1834. Watercolor on paper, 9.2 x 12.8 in. Tate Gallery, London, England.

The Middle Ages

During the Middle Ages (from about AD 500 to 1500 in western Europe), special books known as illuminated manuscripts were made out of parchment paper and illustrated with watercolor paintings by monks who were responsible for making copies of Bible scriptures. They were called illuminated manuscripts because of the incredibly gorgeous illustrations that lit up the books. Some of the paintings were colorful illustrations of Bible stories, and others were ornamental letters. Sometimes the monks took the first letter of text on the page and made it large and ornate, with swoops and swirls, colorful patterns, and pictures inside the letter.

Europe and America

Watercolor painting went in and out of fashion once it came on the scene in Europe and America. At first people thought that watercolor was a sketching medium, only to be used for preliminary studies of large oil paintings. In England, in 1768, a painting society called the Royal Academy of Art was founded in London. They did not consider watercolor to be worthy, and they would only exhibit watercolor paintings by artists who also had oil paintings in the show. Even then, the watercolors were hung in side rooms without good lighting. Watercolor painters quickly got tired of that kind of treatment, and in 1805 they formed their own club so that they could have their own exhibitions.

By 1881, watercolor was very popular and was accepted as a worthy art form by art critics, art collectors, and painting societies.

Turner Changes Everything

In 1799, William Turner was accepted into London's Royal Academy of Art based on the strength of his oil paintings. At the same time, he developed a revolutionary style of watercolor painting that was washy, loose, and abstract. Because Turner was accepted by the Royal Academy, this gave a green light to other artists who wanted to use loose, experimental styles.

No other artistic medium has undergone such scrutiny. Even after watercolor was considered acceptable, it was still regulated for centuries.

MEMBERSHIP REQUIRED
Isn't it absurd that in the world of art, where most people now believe that any painting style is worth doing, there were once restrictions?

The Artist's Materials

Watercolor paint is made of ground-up pigment, water, and a sticky liquid called gum arabic.

Pigments

Pigments are colored materials that are ground to a fine powder. The earliest pigments were made from materials as simple as ground rocks or clay. Some pigments come from gemstones or from animal sources. Many modern pigments are chemicals created in the laboratory.

Gum Arabic

Gum arabic is a water-soluble sap produced by a species of the acacia tree, which grows in Africa. When the liquid dries, the pigment is bound to the painting surface by the gum arabic. Even so, watercolors are very delicate and vulnerable to light and moisture. Because of this, most watercolor artists frame their best paintings, placing glass in front of the image.

Watercolor Cakes

Watercolor paint in its dried cake form is sometimes called a "pan." You have eight pans in your kit.

TIP To get rich color out of dried watercolor pans, drop some clean water on them using the eyedropper. Give the water several minutes to dissolve some of the pigments. You can also rub the top of the cake vigorously with your brush to get more of the pigment to dissolve.

Palette

The palette in your kit holds your watercolor pans and has several wells for mixing colors. If you need a bigger palette, you can use an old, white dinner plate (ask your parents first) or anything flat with a smooth, shiny surface.

CLEANING YOUR PALETTE

Keeping your palette clean helps you mix pure colors. A great way to do this is with a moist paper towel. If you don't feel like cleaning the entire palette, you can use your paper towel to wipe out just one well. If you want it to be absolutely sparkling clean, you can remove the watercolor pans and wash the whole thing in hot, soapy water.

Watercolor Pencils

Watercolor pencils are made out of dried watercolor, similar to what is in the watercolor cakes. You can sharpen watercolor pencils just like you would a regular pencil. There are four watercolor pencils in your kit.

 TIP Use a glass jar or plastic tub for your water jar, or try using an ice-cube tray. Each "cube" can be used to rinse off a different color of paint. Your water will stay cleaner longer.

Eyedropper

The eyedropper can be used to drop clean water directly on the watercolor cakes, to fill up a well with water before you start to dilute color, or to take a few drops of a premixed color to begin a new color mix in a different well.

Sponge

Your sponge can be used for creating texture in your painting, removing excess water from your painting, or cleaning your palette.

Paper

There are ten sheets of paper in your portfolio to get you started. Once you've experimented with regular paper, you may choose to get special watercolor paper. It is available at art supply stores and comes in different thicknesses and textures.

Tray

Use the custom-designed painting tray as a work surface. It will contain all the messy, watery paints as you work. It's also a place to leave your painting as it dries. The wet paper will stick to the tray, so your masterpieces will dry as flat as possible.

Additional Materials

- WATER
- WATER JAR
- PAPER TOWELS
- 2B (SOFT) PENCIL
- RULER
- SCRAP PAPER
- WHITE CRAYON
- PHOTOGRAPHS
- NATURE SPECIMEN
- MIRROR

Brushes and Techniques

Watercolor artists choose their brushes based on how much spring they have and how well they hold a point.

How Much Spring?

The amount a brush tip bounces back after being pressed into the paper is called "spring." It is determined by the type of hairs in the brush, not the size of the brush. Brushes made with synthetic hairs, like the ones in your kit, have a lot of spring to them.

NATURAL HAIRS
A favorite (although very expensive) brush of artists is the Kolinsky sable brush. Its hair is taken from the tails of Siberian minks, so it comes to a natural point.

What's the Point?

All round watercolor brushes taper toward the tip to form a point. Brushes made from natural hairs (collected from animals) come to a natural point because each and every hair is tapered.

Large Round Brush

This is the most versatile of the three brushes in your kit. It is large but also has a small point, so it can be used for a range of brushstroke sizes.

Flat Brush

This can be used for painting larger areas or making square brush marks.

Small Round Brush

This can be used to make small marks and for adding details when finishing a painting.

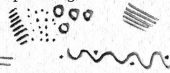

CARING FOR YOUR BRUSHES
After every painting session, rinse off your brushes and lay them out flat to dry or place them brush-side up in your empty water jar. Never leave them standing on their hairs in the jar—this can result in permanently bent hairs, making your brushes unusable. If you aren't planning to use your brushes again for some time, you can wash the hairs out with soap.

Using Watercolor Pencils

Watercolor pencils are a great way to experiment with watercolors because you're probably more accustomed to using a pencil than a paintbrush. They're also a little easier to control than liquid paint.

Here are some of the ways you can use your pencils:

• Apply dry pencil over dry watercolor to add detail to a painting or create texture.

• Dip the tip of a pencil in water to make bold lines over dry watercolor.

• Using your brush and clean water, you can blend pencil lines.

Wax Crayon Resist

You can make wax resists with a white crayon. This technique is handy for making sure that a white object in your painting stays white and doesn't get any other paint on it.

TIP Draw on your paper with a white crayon, pressing hard. When you paint over the crayon wax, the watercolor will not stick to the area where you drew, leaving a white mark. This is called wax resist because the wax resists the water.

Texture

Your sponge can be used for creating texture in your painting, removing excess water from your painting, or cleaning your palette.

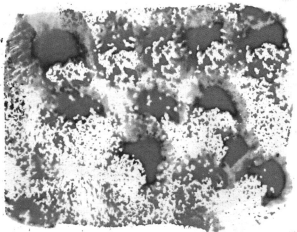

You can create a texture like this by using the sponge in your kit to apply blue watercolor over a rectangle of yellow watercolor.

TIP To make texture with your sponge, mix a color on your palette, dip the sponge into the paint, and then dab it onto your painting. Or, dip your sponge right onto the watercolor cake for more intense color. You can use this technique to add details to rocks, grass, the side of a house, or to an abstract painting.

The Color Wheel

CIRCLE OF COLOR
The color wheel consists of 12 colors: three primary colors, three secondary colors, and six tertiary colors.

The color wheel is a circular arrangement of colors that painters use to help them mix the colors they want and to think about palette choices. A color wheel is like a circular rainbow, where every color has a specific place. Depending on its position, each color relates to the other colors in its own special way.

Primary Colors

The primary colors are red, yellow, and blue. These colors are special because they can be used to create all other colors. However, there is no way to make a primary color from any other colors.

Secondary Colors

Orange, green, and violet are the three secondary colors. Each one is formed by combining two primary colors. Mixing red and yellow together makes orange, mixing blue and yellow makes green, and mixing red and blue makes violet.

Tertiary Colors

There are six tertiary colors: red-orange, yellow-orange, yellow-green, blue-green, blue-violet, and red-violet. Each one is formed by mixing a primary color with a neighboring secondary color.

Warm and Cool Colors

If you divide the color wheel straight down the middle between the violets and the yellows, you are separating the warm and cool colors. Warm colors are red, red-violet, oranges, and yellows. Cool colors are blues, blue-violet, and greens.

TRY COMPLEMENTS

Have you ever wondered why red and green are the "official" colors of Christmas? It's a good bet that one of the reasons is that they make a complementary pair. If you are looking to add some dazzle to your painting, try placing complements side by side.

USING NEUTRALS

Neutrals are the most common colors in our environment. Some examples of neutral colors are: the brown of a tree trunk, the gray of a thick fog, the soft yellow of an ear of corn, and the hazy blue of the sky at the horizon's edge.

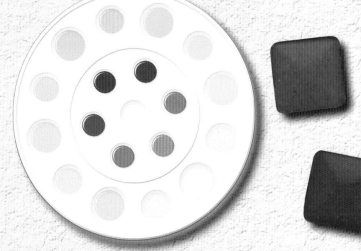

Complementary Colors

If you draw an arrow straight across the center of the color wheel from one color to another, it will be pointing at a complementary color. The basic complementary pairs are: red and green, blue and orange, and violet and yellow. Because these colors are so different from each other, they can cause an intense shimmer when placed next to each other in a painting.

Neutral Colors

If you mix two colors that are direct opposites, you will create a neutral color. Grays, browns, and earth tones are examples of neutral colors. If you mix complementary colors in just the right ratio, you will create gray.

Color Mixing

The Flower

In this exercise, you will get a simple introduction to color mixing, both on your palette and on your paper. It's fun to do if you've never mixed a color before—or even if you're a pro.

1 Start with the Primaries

Imagine there is a triangle on your sheet of paper. Paint a blobby, circular shape of red at one point, yellow at another, and blue at the last one. Use about equal amounts of paint for each blob. Clean your brush after painting each color. To get all of the pigment out, press your brush against the water jar a few times as you are rinsing it.

2 Make the Complements

With a clean, wet brush, mix the red and the yellow together right on your paper. Did you get orange?

After rinsing your brush again, do the same with the yellow and blue, then the blue and red. You should get green and violet.

3 Now Make Gray

Mix all the colors together in the middle to get your neutral grays and browns.

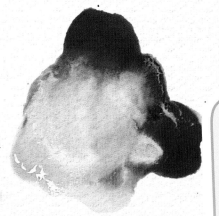

TIP You have all of these colors in your palette, but now you know how to make them—and their variations—from scratch.

Color Grid Exercise:
Getting to Know Your Colors

The purpose of this exercise is to help you get to know your colors. By overlapping transparent layers of each of your watercolor cake colors, you will see how their transparent layers interact. Where the stripes of the grid cross, a new color will be created. This is a way of mixing colors on your paper instead of on your palette.

1 Create the Grid

Use a pencil to draw a grid on your paper. Measure out six bands that are each 6 inches long, ½ inch wide, and ¼ inch apart.

On each band, write the name of the color you will paint there. You'll only use six of your eight colors: red, orange, yellow, green, blue, and black.

Using your flat brush, paint an even-toned horizontal stripe of each color.

Allow the piece to dry completely.

2 Explore the Colors

Now paint the bands of color in the other direction.

What colors have you mixed by allowing the transparent layers to interact?

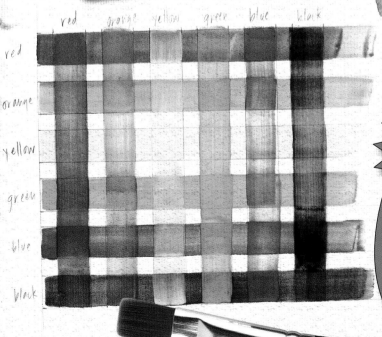

(!) TRANSPARENCY OF WATERCOLOR

When you work with watercolor, you will notice that the colors that look bright and dark when they are wet on your paper become much lighter when they dry. So light, in fact, that you can see the paper through the color. This phenomenon of being able to see the paper through the color is called transparency. Experienced watercolorists try to preserve transparency in their paintings. They do this by building up colors slowly in multiple layers and letting the white of the paper shine through. A painting that shows this effect is often described as being "luminous."

Expressionism

Paul Klee is often called an Expressionist. Expressionist painters use symbols, bright colors, shapes, and playful arrangements of objects to describe their thoughts and emotions. For example, in the painting *Versunkene Landschaft* (*Sunken Landscape*), the flower might symbolize the artist's feelings of happiness or of a personal blossoming. So, Klee may have painted the flower as a means of expressing feelings that he was having. That's different from looking at a real flower and painting it.

Paul Klee, *Versunkene Landschaft*, 1918. Watercolor over pen, 6.9 x 6.4 in. Museum Folkwang Essen, Germany.

Carol Mansfield, *Sunflower*, 2000. Graphite pencil and acrylic on board, 15 x 20 in.

Symbolic Sunflower

Like Paul Klee, Carol Mansfield creates Expressionistic works, but her paintings have a much different style. Her painting *Sunflower* expresses the feelings, colors, and energy of summer. Instead of depicting exactly what a sunflower looks like, she employs a symbolic sunflower to evoke the feelings of the warm summer months. Her painting is experimental in her use of lines, patterns, and swooping brushstrokes. She also uses acrylic paints, which, like watercolors, can be mixed with water. However, some watercolor societies do not allow acrylic paintings into their exhibitions because they are not "true" watercolors.

Paul Klee, Expressing Himself

Paul Klee was an artist who loved to experiment with color. He imagined that nature was made of building blocks of color and depicted that in his work, which is why many of his paintings look like playful versions of the grid exercise we just did.

Klee grew up in a musical family, and some people say they can see that influence in the flowing patterns in his paintings. He used a great variety of techniques to fill his paintings with bright colors, patterns, and experimental textures. He didn't follow any strict rules about where things should go in a picture, so he could place objects up, down, and all around in his compositions. As a result, his paintings express a dreamy playfulness. When you look at paintings like *Versunkene Landschaft*, it seems like Klee was always lighthearted and cheerful.

14

"One eye sees, the other feels."
—Paul Klee

Acrylic or Watercolor:
What's the Difference?

Although acrylics and watercolors have a lot in common, some watercolorists look down their noses at painters who use acrylics. Why? Because with acrylic paint you can cover up your mistakes. Acrylic paints are made with the same pigments as watercolors and can be mixed with water just like watercolors, but there is one ingredient that is different: the binder. In watercolor paint, the binder is gum arabic. In acrylic paint, the binder is an acrylic polymer emulsion, which is a lot like white craft glue.

Watercolor

Acrylic

When the polymer emulsion dries, it is like a layer of clear plastic and is no longer soluble in water. This allows you to paint one layer of acrylic paint over another without the layers mixing at all. With watercolors, the gum arabic is always water-soluble, even after it dries, so if you paint one layer over another, the colors mix. Too many layers and you've got what watercolorists call "mud."

"Mud" results when several colors mix to create a murky, yucky gray.

15

Experimenting with Expressionism

This exercise will incorporate playful techniques to make a lively, bright, and textured abstract painting in the style of Paul Klee's *Versunkene Landschaft*.

Materials

- SCRAP PAPER
- PENCIL
- WHITE CRAYON
- PAPER
- WATER JAR
- WATER
- WATERCOLOR PAINTS
- BRUSHES
- WATERCOLOR PENCILS
- PAPER TOWELS

PHOTOS

OF FLOWERS!

PHOTO OF YOUR HOME!

1 Pick a Theme

Think of a theme for your picture. In our example, the theme is "home." You could choose a part of your life, like school or friends, or you could pick an aspect of the world, like a season or a place.

2 Make a List of Symbols

Make a list of words that represent what you feel and imagine. Your list can include anything related to your theme. For our theme of "home," the list includes: house, dog, tree, fun, bright, flower, and sunshine. Choose one of your words. You'll have a chance to draw your other picture symbols later in this exercise, but here are some examples.

What do you see in your mind?

What feelings do you get when you think of your theme?

3 Wax Resist

Now it's time to start painting. Choose an item from your list of symbols. It could be the largest item or your favorite item on the list. "House" is the word chosen for our example. With a white crayon, draw a picture of that item in the center of your paper. (The crayon marks will be a little hard to see at this point.) Paint some blocks of color with your flat brush, using the technique of "saving the edges" (see below) to keep your colors pure. Allow everything to dry before you move on to the next step.

SAVING THE EDGES

Saving the edges is a way to work quickly in watercolor without having to let things dry between colors. This technique is great for recording impressions of a place or a memory when you don't have time to build up layers or add details. To keep your wet colors from blending into other colors placed nearby, "save" a strip of white between every shape.

See how saving the edges keeps the colors separate and pure?

What kinds of colors are created when washes overlap?

4 Add More Washes

When you spread paint smoothly over a broad area, it's called a wash. You created some washes in step three. See what happens when you add some washes over the previous colors. Make sure they have dried first! While your washes are drying, practice drawing symbols of your other words on some scrap paper.

Tip To speed up drying time between washes, you can use a hair dryer. To prevent your paper from blowing away, point the dryer straight down from above your painting. If you blow from the side, your painting will flip over and the wet colors will run.

5 More Symbols

Choose some of your picture symbols to add to your painting using watercolor pencils and your large and small round brushes.

In our example, one of the orange washes was made into a tree trunk by using a watercolor pencil and green paint to make leaves on the top. Flowers, a dog, sunshine, colorful windows, and more trees in the background were also added.

Finished!

TIP Use your watercolor pencils and your sponge to add texture to your painting. See page 9 for techniques and ideas.

! DETAIL AND TEXTURE
In our example, there is "bark" on the tree (created with brown watercolor pencil), "grass" made with the sponge, and some other lines added to give the painting more color, detail, and texture.

Other Approaches to Expressionism

Mike Nailer

What feelings or ideas do you think Mike Nailer is expressing in this painting? Perhaps she is expressing a feeling of excitement or the idea of spring. Do these ideas go together? Can you come up with a story behind this painting? Her technique is loose and experimental. Do you notice how the light green spots are layered over the pink shape? This is possible because she uses gouache.

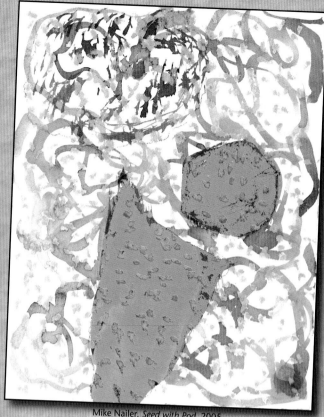

Mike Nailer, *Seed with Pod*, 2005.
Watercolor and gouache on paper, 8 x 6 in.

WATERCOLOR VS. GOUACHE

Gouache is a paint that is similar to watercolor, but it has white mixed into it. The white pigment is actually made out of chalk. This makes it possible to cover one color with another, because white is opaque and you can't see through it. In this way, gouache is like acrylic paint, but it doesn't dry to a plastic, undissolvable layer like acrylic. When gouache dries, it can be dissolved again in water.

Al Mulkey, *Once*, 2001.
Watercolor on paper, 1.5 x 7.25 in.

Al Mulkey

What do you think this colorful painting by Al Mulkey is expressing? The bright colors have a joyful, exuberant feeling, and the squiggly shapes give it a sense of playfulness. The long, horizontal shape of the painting suggests that there is a story behind it, perhaps a memory of a day, an emotion, or an imagined event. To keep his colors pure, Mulkey used the "saving the edges" technique you learned in the Expressionism exercise. He uses a range of both warm and cool colors, varying the mixtures from light to dark.

EXPRESSIONISM OR ABSTRACTION? WHAT'S THE DIFFERENCE?

The difference between these two approaches is that one comes from the inside and the other from the outside.

THE EXPRESSIONIST ARTIST . . .

has an idea or a feeling and tries to put that feeling onto the paper. He or she doesn't necessarily care about picturing anything that exists in the external, or "real," world but might use something real as a symbol to help describe a feeling.

THE ABSTRACT ARTIST . . .

sees an object or a scene in the real world and tries to depict that in a bold and simple way. He or she peels away details to get down to the essence of a scene. Sometimes, an abstract painting can inspire an emotion in someone who views it, but the subject of the painting was outside of the artist.

Of course, these approaches often overlap. In your paintings, you might use a little of both, getting inspired by ideas inside you and also by beautiful subjects that are outside of you.

Landscapes

To "abstract" means to remove or take something away. In abstract art, the thing that is removed is the specific, exact visual information, like what you would see if you looked through a camera lens at a particular scene. What is left after taking away the specifics of the scene is the universal quality of that scene, such as a color, a basic bold shape, or a beautiful pattern.

For example, look at these images of a park scene. On the top is the photograph, with all of its details. If you abstract (remove) the details, such as the pattern of the bark, the texture of the rocks and soil on the ground, the green pine trees in the distance, and the individual leaves on the yellow-orange bushes, what you have left is an arrangement of bold shapes.

Georgia O'Keeffe, *Evening Star No. VI*, 1917. Watercolor on paper, 8.9 x 12 in. Georgia O'Keeffe Museum, Santa Fe, New Mexico.

Georgia O'Keeffe, Abstracting Landscapes

In 1916, Georgia O'Keeffe spent some time in Texas, teaching art at West Texas State Normal College (now West Texas A&M) in Canyon, Texas. During this time, she took long walks in the canyons and plains, soaking up the vast expanse of the landscape, the brilliant sunsets, and the intensely bright stars of the night skies. She painted a series of watercolors that were inspired by all of the things she saw. Her style began to move away from realism (showing exactly what the scenes looked like) and toward abstraction (simplifying the image to the underlying forms). In these watercolors, she used colorful, juicy washes of paint, allowing some of the colors to flow together and mix without her control. Though her themes were taken from objects in nature such as an evening star, a canyon, or the sunrise, her feelings of freedom when she thought of the Texas plains pushed her work into the realm of abstract painting. These paintings led to her famous original series of oil paintings depicting beautiful flowers and desert landscapes.

DETAILED PHOTO!

TIP To take this idea further, you could abstract the stripelike shapes of the tree trunks and use their rhythms to make a bold, simple painting of stripes.

"Art is not what you see, but what you make others see."
—Georgia O'Keeffe

Abstracting a Landscape

In this exercise, you will create a painting using simple, powerful shapes derived from what inspires you in nature.

Materials

- LANDSCAPE PHOTO
- SCRAP PAPER
- PENCIL
- WATER JAR
- WATER
- BRUSHES
- PAPER
- PAPER TOWELS

1 Choose a Subject

Choose a photo or imagine a scene that has meaning for you—a place where you like to go to be alone and think, a favorite view, or a spot in nature that inspires you.

IMAGINE

Think about your subject and try to picture it in your mind's eye.

- *What does your imagination remember?*
- *What does it leave out?*
- *What colors do you see?*

2 Make a Simple Sketch

Divide the areas of the scene into simple shapes. On a piece of scratch paper, practice sketching these shapes. Our example is divided into sections of sky, hills, shoreline, and lake.

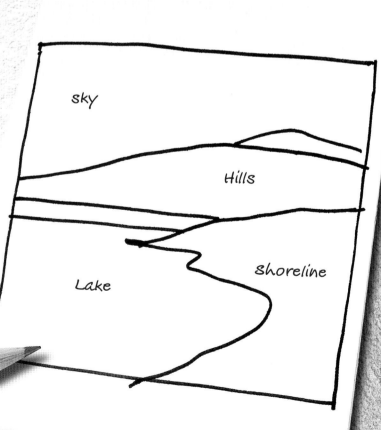

sky

Hills

Lake

Shoreline

3 Wash

Now take your paper and use the "saving the edges" technique you learned in the last exercise. Fill these shapes with bold color. You can leave areas of white open to show clouds in the sky, and to add texture to the foreground.

PALETTE OF COLORS

The word "palette" is also used to describe the color choices an artist makes in painting. For instance, if you were going to paint a picture of the sun, you might choose a palette of yellows and oranges. For a painting of a night scene, you might use a palette of dark purples, blues, and black.

Finished!

WET-ON-WET

In our example, this technique works perfectly for the lake because it has a variety of colors in it. Use this approach to give your landscape extra color and flair.

Other Approaches to Landscape Painting

Karen Lewis

In this painting, the artist focused on the simple circles of light around the glowing streetlights. These shapes are echoed in the circle around the lighthouse and the arcs of light cast onto the paved road. Also, she used just two colors, blue and orange, which are complementary colors on the color wheel. Even though there is quite a bit of delicate detail in this painting, the overall feel is very strong because of the abstract shapes and simple colors.

Karen Lewis, *Hania Lighthouse at Night*, 2001. Watercolor and ink on paper, 5 x 3 in.

Virginia Howlett, *Big Blue 18*, 2005. Watercolor on paper, 21 x 28.5 in.

Virginia Howlett

Virginia Howlett creates beautiful, dreamy paintings of cloudy skies. She uses wet-on-wet techniques, touching a brushful of color to moist paper and letting the paint flow. Do you think her paintings are abstract, Expressionist, or a little of both?

Michael Dickter

This elegant painting of palm trees by Michael Dickter owes its strength to strong, abstract shapes. The background is so simple; it is really just three horizontal stripes. A wide, light blue wash defines the sky, a narrow, darker blue stripe tells us where the water is, and a yellow stripe describes the sandy beach. In front of these stripes arch the slender, swaying palm trees like signatures on a page.

Michael Dickter, *Afternoon View*, 2001. Watercolor on paper, 12 x 9 in.

> **! WET-ON-WET**
> Sometimes, instead of waiting for each layer to dry, you can apply wet paint on top of wet paint or paint directly onto wet paper. This is called the wet-on-wet technique. It is used when you want to represent a variety of colors or if you want to mix colors directly on your painting. This approach is a little unpredictable, so keep your sponge close by to remove any excess water or pigment. The result of wet-on-wet can be soft shapes, blurred edges, or a mix of color.

Nature Studies

One great way to practice your watercolor skills is by doing nature studies. Objects that can be collected outside, like plants, shells, and flowers, can be beautiful and inspiring subjects for a painting. They have the added benefit of sitting still while you paint, so you can paint them over and over, which is terrific practice.

Making nature studies in a notebook is something that scientists and explorers (like Lewis and Clark or John James Audubon) do to keep records of new and interesting things they see. You can also use this technique to pass the time, like a favorite hobby. This is what Beatrix Potter, the beloved author of the Peter Rabbit books, did when she was young.

Beatrix Potter, *Study of Twelve Caterpillars*, 1875. From her drawing book.

THE TALE OF PETER RABBIT

by

BEATRIX POTTER

F. WARNE & C.º LTD

Beatrix Potter, Nature Lover

The young Beatrix Potter spent a lot of time sketching the natural world. She and her brother played outside and entertained themselves by making sketches of everything they saw. They also brought home animals like rabbits, lizards, and frogs, which they kept as pets as well as using them as subjects for their paintings and drawings. The sketch above is a page from a notebook Beatrix kept when she was eight years old. As an adult, Beatrix Potter loved children and often wrote letters to her friends' children, illustrated with pen-and-ink drawings. Her celebrated book, *The Tale of Peter Rabbit,* began as a "picture letter" to the sick little son of her former governess.

"Now run along and don't get into mischief."
—Peter Rabbit's Mum

Studying Nature Close Up

In this exercise, you will make a careful naturalist's study of an object you collect from nature.

Materials

- NATURE SPECIMEN
- PAPER
- PENCIL
- WATER JAR
- WATER
- WATERCOLOR PAINTS
- BRUSHES
- PAPER TOWELS

1 Pick a Subject

Pick a flower or find something on a nature walk that you can take home and study close up, such as a shell or a leaf.

TIP Place your object on a piece of white paper so that it stands out. Set up a desk lamp so that a light shines on it, so you can see the light areas and the shadows.

2 Sketch Outline

Using a 2B (soft) pencil, sketch the outline of your object.

3 Add Shadows

Look for the shadow areas on your object. Darken these with thin layers of black watercolor. Allow the black to dry.

4 Add Light

Where are the light areas? Paint a light wash of yellow over these areas. Let this wash dry.

5 Add Color

What are the main colors in the object? In our flower, there are three main colors: green, yellow, and orange. Paint a light wash of these colors inside your pencil lines and over the top of your blacks and yellows.

6 Add Layers

After the first color washes dry, you might see that they need to be brighter or that they need adjusting. Look closely at your colors to see if they need any variation from what comes directly off of your watercolor cakes. The yellow in our flower is actually a yellow-orange, so a little bit of orange was mixed into the yellow in this step. The green also needed a little bit of orange mixed into it to make it more neutral. Apply layers of the newly mixed colors until they look bright enough. Let each color dry first.

Details!

TIP Now you can use your watercolor pencils to add details, creating marks and lines for texture. It's also fun to write field study notes on your drawing. You can write the name of your subject, when and where it was collected, and any interesting details you can think of.

Other Approaches to Nature Painting

Barbara Creed

This watercolor by Barbara Creed is a page from her garden notebook. In it she makes sketches and writes journal entries about the garden around her house. She loves to gaze at and appreciate the garden she so carefully planted. A great way to look at something you love is to paint it. This is because you start to really see it when you take the time to look at all its details. Is there something you love that you could sketch and write about in your own watercolor journal?

Barbara Ann Creed, *Poppies*, 2002.
Watercolor on paper, 11 x 9 in.

"Great art picks up where nature ends."
—Marc Chagall

MIXING NATURAL COLORS

The colors in your painting kit are very bright. In nature, most colors are toned down from the intensity of the paints in your kit. To mix a less intense color, add a little bit of the color's complement (remember, complementary colors sit across the color wheel from each other).

Llamas in the field - day four

Virginia Howlett, *Yellowstone Llamas*, 2005.
Watercolor on paper, 2 x 3 in.

Virginia Howlett

Virginia Howlett brought her watercolors on a ten-day backpacking trip through Yellowstone National Park. Because watercolors are nice and light, her backpack didn't weigh her down. The backpackers brought llamas to carry the tents and ten days' worth of food. This sketch shows the llamas taking a much-deserved break from their heavy loads.

Travel sketching

Before the camera was invented, artists and travelers brought watercolors with them on their journeys, making paintings to keep a record of what they saw. These days, travelers are used to having a camera and coming home from vacations with stacks of photographs to show to friends.

Can you imagine using only your watercolors to "take pictures" on your next trip? Artist John Singer Sargent did just that. He brought his watercolors on all of his travels. He even planned special painting vacations with his friends who traveled and painted together. He brought watercolors with him—not the oil paints that he was famous for using—because watercolors are lightweight and easy to carry.

John Singer Sargent, *The Grand Canal, Venice*, 1902. Watercolor over graphite on white woven paper, 9.8 x 13.8 in. Fogg Art Museum, Cambridge, Massachusetts.

AMERICAN FRONTIER

During the age of exploration on the American frontier, artists like Thomas Moran carried their watercolors into the uncharted West. Moran traveled to what is now Yellowstone National Park to make watercolor sketches of the geysers, mountains, and gorgeous scenery of the area. His paintings were so stunning that in 1872 Congress voted to make Yellowstone the first national park.

John Singer Sargent's Venice

John Singer Sargent kept a busy schedule in his studio, painting large oil portraits for wealthy patrons. People who sat for a portrait by Sargent were guaranteed to become celebrities afterward. What many people don't know is he really didn't care for the work he was famous for doing. His real love was painting city and nature scenes. He planned summer sketching trips to other countries and into the woods, sometimes accompanied by his special painting friends or his family, and sometimes by himself. He looked forward to these trips all winter as he toiled away on studio portraits. He was especially drawn to Venice, Italy, where he completed this watercolor of the Grand Canal.

"To live in Sargent's watercolors, you will find you have fallen in love with paper and paint."
—Rex Brandt

Thumbnail Sketches

Thumbnail sketches are small sketches that you make quickly to help you decide what to paint. They are so called because they are small, like the nail of your thumb.

Choose a photo or find a scene to inspire your thumbnail sketches. Draw a series of ten small rectangles (1 to 2 inches wide) in pencil on a piece of scrap paper. Looking at the view you are interested in painting, focus on ten different areas of that view. Some can be close-up and detailed; others can be more distant views. Look at the top, right, and left of the scene.

A NEW VIEW

Consider looking at the scene from another angle. You can move your seat to the right or the far left, stand up, or sit very low for a different perspective.

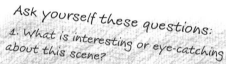

Ask yourself these questions:

1. What is interesting or eye-catching about this scene?

2. What inspires me about this scene?

3. Are there any parts of this scene that I might not have noticed at first?

Thinking in a Grid!

If you are using a photograph, a good way to get started is to think about the photograph in sections. Imagine there are lines dividing the picture into four sections. Divide your sketch into four sections, too. Look at the big shapes and see where they are in relation to your grid.

Out and About

Bring your watercolors on a trip or to your favorite spot in your town or neighborhood. Make a watercolor sketch of the view from a comfortable sitting place, such as a café or a park.

Materials

- PHOTO OR VIEW
- SCRAP PAPER
- PENCIL
- PAPER
- WATER JAR
- WATER
- WATERCOLOR PAINTS
- BRUSHES
- PAPER TOWELS
- WATERCOLOR PENCILS

1 Make Sketches

Find a comfortable spot with a good view of a scene you wish to paint, or choose a photograph from a vacation. Try to pick a view that has simple shapes in it, with light and shadow. Make thumbnail sketches of your chosen scene.

2 Choose a Favorite

Pick your favorite thumbnail sketch and practice drawing a larger version on some scratch paper. When you are ready, make a drawing on the paper you will be using for your painting.

"Painting is just another way of keeping a diary."
—Pablo Picasso

3 Shadow and Light

Look for light and shadow in your view. Apply transparent layers of black for the shadows. Allow your black washes to dry.

ARTISTIC LICENSE

When you are creating a painting, there is no rule that says you have to paint exactly what is there. You can move objects and change colors as much as you want. In our example, the bowl is moved to a spot where it is more visible, and the colors are much brighter than they are in the photograph.

More paint makes darker gray-black. Vary the amount of water and paint to get different shades of gray.

TIP

4 Block in Color

Decide on your main color areas. Block these in with light washes of color. In our example, the lamppost is blue-green, the sidewalk beneath the cat is purple, the water is yellow-green, the brick wall is red-orange, and the trim on the boats is yellow.

31

5 Add Layers of Color

When the first washes are dry, you can deepen your colors with additional layers. Also, look for the sunny areas in your view. You can apply a wash of yellow in these light areas. Allow the new washes to dry.

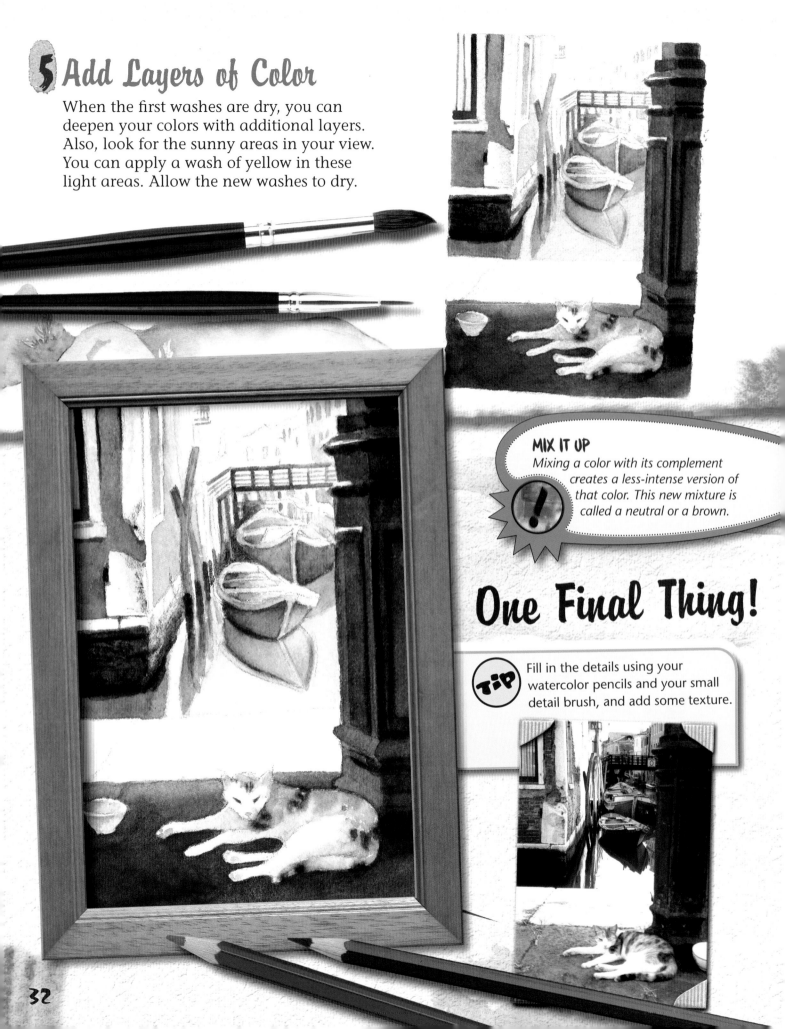

MIX IT UP

Mixing a color with its complement creates a less-intense version of that color. This new mixture is called a neutral or a brown.

One Final Thing!

TIP Fill in the details using your watercolor pencils and your small detail brush, and add some texture.

Other Approaches to Travel Sketching

Barbara Creed

Barbara Creed made this sketch on a watercolor postcard. You can buy packs of postcard-sized watercolor paper at your local art supply store. One side of the card is blank, and the other is printed with areas for the note, address, and stamp. They are great for carrying along on trips so that you can send a very special greeting back to your friends and family. Creed liked this one so much that she couldn't bear to give it away; instead, she keeps it in a journal of her travels. Her technique is to place bright dabs of intense color around the painting, enhancing it with subtle ink lines after the paint dries.

Barbara Ann Creed, *Sunset at Monument Valley*, 2004.
Watercolor and ink on paper, 3.5 x 4.5 in.

Michael Dickter

Michael created this sketch with watercolor pencils. He painted page after page of quick impressions in a notebook that he carried with him on a trip through Europe. On visits to monuments, museums, parks, and coffee shops in several countries, he sketched, drew, and wrote in his notebook.

Michael Dickter, *Eiffel Tower*, 1986.
Watercolor pencil on paper, 7 x 4 in.

! MAKING CLOUDS

Travel sketching often involves painting clouds. First make a square of sky blue wash on your paper. Use an amount of water in your wash that will leave your paper moist but not flooded with water. With a tissue, paper towel, or a clean sponge, dab an area of the blue to remove some of the blue pigment.

TIP

If you use a paper towel, you can fold it to make sharp edges. This is useful if you are removing color to illustrate harder-edged objects in your painting, like the top of a roof, a sidewalk, or the edge of a table.

33

Portraits

What is the first subject you think of when you sit down to draw or paint? For many artists, it's a person. They may choose to portray their parents, friends, brothers and sisters, or even themselves. Portrait painting is something that is always available to do because we are so often surrounded by people. And if you are by yourself, all you need is a mirror to make a self-portrait!

Mary Cassatt was one of a very small number of women who were able to pursue a career in painting in the 1800s. She's not only a famous portrait painter, but one of the best known female artists in history.

Like Beatrix Potter, Mary Cassatt was fond of children. She chose to capture her favorite subjects—women and children—in casual poses or everyday activities rather than the stiff portrait style of the day. This photo portrait of Cassatt shows how a portrait at the time was typically meant to capture the likeness of a person in a formal rather than casual pose.

Mary Cassatt, *Self-portrait*, c.1880. Watercolor on paper, 13 x 9.6 in. Smithsonian Institution, National Portrait Gallery, Washington, D.C.

Mary Cassatt, Reflecting on Herself

This self-portrait is one of the few watercolors painted by Mary Cassatt. She tended to use oil paints, but she chose watercolor for this piece. Perhaps this is because she was recording a private moment by herself and wanted to use a medium that felt lighter and more personal. Her oil paintings illustrated other peoples' lives, and many were shown in public as part of large exhibitions. With watercolors, she could paint quickly and easily on paper, then put the sketch away in a book or a box, where she didn't have to show it to anyone.

"Every time I paint a portrait, I lose a friend."
—John Singer Sargent

Tips for Drawing Faces

Here are some tips for measuring faces and placing the features in the right spots.

 Tip If you draw these lines in pencil, you can erase them later.

Set It Up

- Draw an oval shape.
- Divide the oval in half horizontally (1).
- Divide that space in half (2).
- Divide the bottom space in half (3).
- Divide the oval in half vertically (4).

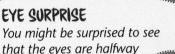

EYE SURPRISE
You might be surprised to see that the eyes are halfway down the face. This leaves room for the forehead and hairline.

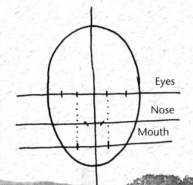

- Divide each side of the top line into thirds. This is where the eyes will go.
- Draw two diagonal notches on both sides of the second line to place the nostrils.
- Draw a dotted line from the top line's inside marks down to the bottom line to find the corners of the mouth.

Add the Features

- On the top line, draw two small ovals for the eyes, with eyebrows above them.
- On the middle line, draw curves outside of the notches to become nostrils.
- On the bottom line, draw the lips between the guideline notches.
- For the hairline, make a notch halfway between the top of the head and the top line. Draw the ears between the top and middle lines.

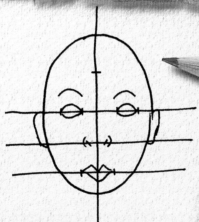

Tip Adjust the shapes of the features, and add hair and other details to give your portrait some personality.

THE FACE OF A CHILD
A child's face has different proportions than an adult's.

- *Divide the oval into seven parts (instead of four parts as you did for the adult face).*
- *Place the line for the eyes on the third mark from the bottom of the oval.*
- *Make the eyes bigger in proportion to the whole face.*
- *Place the features as you did before but arrange them more toward the bottom of the oval.*

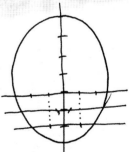

Painting a Portrait

In Mary Cassatt's self-portrait, you can see that she is holding a pad of paper in front of her. She painted this portrait in front of a mirror. You can do your portrait in front of a mirror, or you can use a photograph. Our example is painted from a photograph.

Materials

- PHOTO, MIRROR, OR MODEL
- SKETCHING OR SCRAP PAPER
- PENCIL
- PAPER
- WATER JAR
- WATER
- PAPER TOWELS
- WATERCOLOR PAINTS
- WATERCOLOR PENCILS
- BRUSHES

1 Make a Sketch

With a pencil, sketch in the shape of the head and shoulders. You might want to practice on some scrap paper first. Add the features and some details.

2 Paint the Shadows

Look for the shadows on the face. What color are they? In our example, the shadows look warm. A reddish-purple (with just a little bit of yellow added to make it less intense) was perfect for warm, summertime shadows.

TiP To paint hair, think of it in chunks, not individual strands.

3 Add Color

Cover the main color areas with light washes of color. The skin in our photograph looks like a combination of pink and orange, so a light layer of pink was a good color to start with. For the hair, a layer of yellow-orange matched the highlights.

> **TiP** Whether you work with a mirror or from a photo, leave out details you don't like or don't need.

Mixing Skin Tones

To make skin tones, mix warm colors with a tiny bit of their complements. Use a piece of scrap paper to experiment with the colors you mix. In your painting, create rich tones by layering several thin washes of color.

For an olive complexion, start with yellow and add small amounts of purple and orange.

For a dark complexion, start with orange and add blue, yellow, and red.

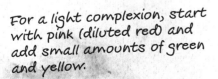

For a light complexion, start with pink (diluted red) and add small amounts of green and yellow.

4 Add More Layers

Give a light wash of yellow to the sunny areas. On the face, apply the yellow wash over all areas except the white highlights on the nose and cheek. In our example, the yellow mixes with the earlier layer of pink and creates a soft skin color.

Be careful not to "lose" white highlights. You can use a white crayon to save these areas.

The Finished Piece!

TIP Deepen colors by adding extra layers of paint, letting each layer dry. Add detail with your small brush or with your watercolor pencils.

Other Approaches to Portrait Painting

Al Mulkey

Do you recognize this face? It's a famous person from American history.

In this portrait, Al Mulkey has reduced everything to a pattern of squares in just one color, sepia, a reddish-brown often used in photography. It is an experiment he conducted to see how far he could simplify a portrait while still having the painting be recognizable as a particular person. To make this painting, he selected a photograph, drew lines on it in a grid pattern, then created the same grid on his watercolor paper. When he went to paint each square, he asked himself, "How dark is this square, overall?" All he painted was light and dark squares, and it still looks like a portrait. Isn't that amazing?

Al Mulkey, *Mr. Lincoln*, 2003.
Watercolor on paper, 5 x 3 in.

Pirjo Berg

Pirjo Berg painted this watercolor from life. This means that she had a model pose for her. The model was draped in colorful, patterned fabrics that Berg represented by using quick, skilled brushstrokes. Could you ask a friend or family member to sit for you? Do you think you'd prefer to paint from life or from a photo?

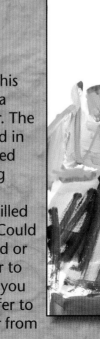

Pirjo Berg, *Kate*, 2002.
Watercolor on paper, 5.5 x 7.5 in.

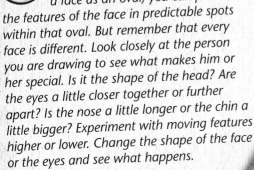

EVERY FACE IS UNIQUE

If you think about the shape of a face as an oval, you can place the features of the face in predictable spots within that oval. But remember that every face is different. Look closely at the person you are drawing to see what makes him or her special. Is it the shape of the head? Are the eyes a little closer together or further apart? Is the nose a little longer or the chin a little bigger? Experiment with moving features higher or lower. Change the shape of the face or the eyes and see what happens.

Take It Anywhere

After completing the five projects in this book, you should have a good idea about what you can do with watercolors. But what's next? First of all, there is a lot of practice to be done. Many watercolor painters practice for years before they feel they have mastered the art of watercolor, which is widely considered to be a difficult and unforgiving medium. Other artists find it easy and freeing. What do you think?

"If I could say it in words, there would be no reason to paint."
—Edward Hopper

Now that you are beginning your journey, where do you think you will go? You might be surprised and come up with a totally new painting technique, or you might master the technique of a famous artist. Your watercolors can lead you to discover new and colorful experiences in your room, or they can accompany you when you explore the world outside. Either way, you will be able to enjoy the freedom of this medium.

Remember, you can take it anywhere!